I0159439

A PATIENT/FAMILY

POCKET GUIDE

FOR

"POST ACUTE"

PATIENT CARE

GAVIN S. JOHNSON   LPN, PR, BA

Name:

Telephone Number:

Address:

©2013 Gavin S. Johnson

This pocket guide contains general information about various post-acute care (PAC) settings. The information is not medical advice and should not be treated as such.

For speaking engagements, media and general inquiries, and group purchases, visit
www.mypostacutePG.com
gavinsjohnson@facebook.com
gavinsjohnson@cox.net

ISBN: 978-0-9796781-9-6

G143 Productions LLC
4101 Delaware Ave #10
Kenner, LA 70065

Printed in the United States of America

MEDICATION TRACKER

MEDICATION:
Dosage:
Time to take medication: AM   PM
Prescription Refill #
Pharmacist:

MEDICATION:
Dosage:
Time to take medication: AM   PM
Prescription Refill #
Pharmacist:

SURGICAL HISTORY

Procedure:
Date:
Surgeon's Name:
Telephone:

Procedure:
Date:
Surgeon's Name:
Telephone:

NEXT APPOINTMENTS

Date-Day-Time:
Doctor/Phone:

Date-Day-Time:
Doctor/Phone:

Date-Day-Time:
Doctor/Phone:

Date-Day-Time:
Doctor/Phone:

Date-Day-Time:
Doctor/Phone:

Date-Day-Time:
Doctor/Phone:

TABLE OF CONTENTS

INTRODUCTION   1

1 | AFTER THE ER....   3

2 | WHAT IS AN LTAC HOSPITAL?   5

3 | ACUTE INPATIENT REHABILITATION
    FACILITIES   11

4 | DAD HAS TO GO TO A "SNIFF?"   15

5 | ON THE ROAD TO RECOVERY...
    OUTPATIENT REHABILITATION   17

6 | MOM CAN GO HOME WITH HOME
    HEALTH? WHAT'S THAT?   19

7 | GRAMMY HAS TO GO TO A NURSING
    HOME NOW?   21

8 | HOSPICE... IS IT REALLY THE END OF
    THE ROAD?   23

9 | ANOTHER OPTION? ASSISTED LIVING   25

Glossary   27

Appendix   29

INTRODUCTION

Hello. My name is Gavin Johnson, and I have been in the healthcare industry for over ten years as a nurse and clinical liaison for an LTAC hospital (I know, what is that?). I even worked as a nurse in a prison during a couple of hurricanes. I have seen strange medical situations and talked to thousands of patients and hundreds of families over the years, and there is one thing that remains the same: Most patients and their family members have no idea why they, Grandma Betty, or Uncle Bobby have to go to an LTACH, SNF (pronounced "sniff"), Home Health, Hospice, Inpatient Acute Rehab, Outpatient Rehab, Nursing Home, or any other "hospital" while they are already in the hospital... Confused?

Most people are, and the purpose of the *pocket guide* is to give the patient and their family an easy-to-understand guide to the next level of care after a trip to the ER (emergency room) or after spending a few days in the hospital.

This *pocket guide* will provide a simple but effective breakdown of where a patient has to go in order to continue their recovery and why. Also, this *pocket guide* will help family members understand why their loved one is going to the next level of care and help them to spread the word to other family members and friends.

1
AFTER THE ER....

Most of us have been there before.... We have either had to bring a family member to the emergency room, gotten the call that Grandpa is in an ambulance on the way to the hospital, or have met family at the ER and walked over to the ICU to see our loved ones hanging on for dear life. In many cases, our loved ones become stable and move from the ICU to a "med surg" unit or some lower level of care within the hospital.

After numerous tests, IVs, shots, and a few days on the "med surg" unit, the doctor comes in and tells the patient and family that Grandpa has to go to an "LTACH" for a few weeks. Then he closes the chart and walks out of the room. Next, the social worker or case manager comes in and gives you or the patient a list of different LTACH hospitals from which to choose. Usually at this point, everybody—including the patient—is confused and wondering, *What is an LTAC hospital?*

2
WHAT IS AN LTAC HOSPITAL?

There are numerous misunderstandings when it comes to healthcare and its different levels. One frequently misunderstood health care option is the Long Term Acute Care Hospital, or LTACH. This is a specialized care hospital designed to treat patients who are very ill. These can be trauma/MVA (motor vehicle accident) victims and/or medically complex individuals who require a few more weeks of specialized hospital care (approximately twenty-five days on average).

WHERE ARE LTACHS LOCATED?

Many LTACHs are found within an acute care hospital and are known in the healthcare industry as HIHs (hospital in/within hospitals) but function independently from the host hospital. LTACHs also exist as freestanding hospitals. All LTACHs provide a vital service to their patients offering **specialized** treatments that are more cost effective and streamlined specifically to the patient's needs.

IS AN LTAC THE SAME AS A NURSING HOME OR REHABILITATION FACILITY?

Long Term Acute Care Hospitals are *not* the same as nursing homes or rehab facilities. The main difference is that an LTACH, which is licensed as an acute care hospital, has full-time registered nurses and doctors on staff and treat critically sick patients on ventilators, dialysis, or with many other medical conditions. Nursing homes do **NOT** have doctors seeing their patients daily and are not equipped to perform routine procedures and tests.

In general, LTACHs are equipped to provide the same level of care and most services that "STACHs" or Short Term Acute Care Hospitals can provide.

WHAT DO LTACHS DO?

LTACHs are specialized to treat severely ill patients who would *benefit* from prolonged care (typically 2 -4 weeks). They generally provide the same care services as a normal hospital, although there are a few exceptions. For example, LTACHs do not have ERs or pediatric, gynecological, and obstetric services.

WHAT IS THE TYPICAL TYPE OF PATIENT SEEN IN AN LTACH?

The most commonly seen patients in an LTACH include the following:

1. Ventilator patients who will require prolonged weaning time. Usually, they have a new tracheostomy and would go to an LTACH for "vent weaning."

2. ESRD (End Stage Renal Disease) requiring ongoing dialysis.

3. Multiple IV antibiotic therapies, other IV medications, or blood transfusions.

4. Complex wound care and multiple decubitus ulcers.

WHY DO WE NEED LTACHS?

Long Term Acute Care Hospitals were created in the 1980s and are needed because they help free up beds in acute hospitals. From ERs, ICUs, and CCUs to telemetry units, having beds available at all times is needed for communities of all sizes. This is especially true in heavily populated cities. For example, if a natural disaster or an outbreak of disease were to occur in a community or city, most people would go to their local emergency room and would be admitted, in most cases. If the beds in this hospital are full, the public would be left without, or the system would be severely stressed. For this reason, LTACHs are designed to care for the sick patients who require extended acute care and recovery time.

WHY CAN'T I STAY IN THE HOSPITAL UNTIL I'M READY TO GO HOME?

Our healthcare system has been set up to pay hospitals according to the illness that the patient has. Medicare and most insurance companies only pay the hospitals a certain amount based on the condition being treated. If the patient requires further treatment, they are required to transfer the patient or seek the next level of care (such as an LTACH, SNF (Skilled Nursing Facility), or one of the items mentioned in the beginning of the guide.

*** In late 2012 into 2013, the term "Transitional Care Hospitals" began to replace the term "LTACH." If you see or hear this term, it refers to the same type of facility***

Here is a typical scenario that a patient or family might see, which would result in a future LTACH admission:

Grandma Betty—a seventy-four-year-old who has a history of COPD, diabetes, hypertension, and arthritis—is at home getting 2 liters of oxygen through nasal cannula. She gets up to go to the bathroom and unfortunately falls and breaks her right hip. Uncle Bobby finds her down a couple of hours later, and she goes to the ER. After surgery to repair her broken hip, she is having trouble getting off of the ventilator (due to her history of COPD). After eight days of attempted ventilator weaning, the pulmonologist has decided that Grandma need to get a "trach" due to her prolonged ventilator situation to relieve the stress of the "vent" tube in her throat area and to help with her recovery.

She successfully gets her "trach" and is stable. The MDs then talk to the family about transferring Grandma to an "LTACH" for vent weaning; physical, occupational, speech, and swallow therapy; IV medications for pain and infection; and wound care for her right hip surgical incision.

There are numerous other scenarios in which a patient may find themselves in need of an LTACH, but the one described is fairly common.

In conclusion, LTACHs do provide a vital service to the patient population that require an extended recovery time, and we all want our loved ones to get the best and most appropriate medical care for their particular illness.

QUESTIONS

_____

_____

_____

_____

NOTES

_____

_____

_____

_____

3
ACUTE INPATIENT REHABILITATION FACILITIES

Acute Inpatient Rehabilitation Facilities or "IRFs" typically provide care for the next level of patients. A diverse treatment team is put together to assist patients in potentially reaching their recovery goals and achieving the highest quality of life. The goal is to have the patient resume their ADLs (activities of daily living), work, school, or recreational activities in a manner that is as close to normal as possible.

The top three medical diagnoses of rehabilitation patients are as follows:

1) Stroke/CVA: 50%
2) Head Injuries: 10%
3) Brain Hemorrhage/Injuries: 7%

Age ranges for Rehabilitation patients:
1) 80 yrs and older: 23%
2) 70-79 yrs old: 28%

3) 60-69 yrs old: 19%
4) 50-59 yrs old: 13%
5) 30-49 yrs old: 12%

Typically, these patients have suffered a stroke or brain injury but are on the road to recovery and are past the critical phase. They require intensive rehab but do not have all of the other medical issues that an "LTACH" patient has. In many cases, patients will have a speech therapist who will work closely with the doctor and patient on evaluating and treating the individuals with communication and swallowing problems resulting from a stroke, brain injury, or other neurological event. Physical and Occupation Therapists will be a part of the patient's intensive recovery team as well. In many cases, there will be frequent group therapy treatments, and many facilities provide rehabilitation treatments on the weekends, with family involvement.

HOW LONG WILL I BE AT THE REHAB FACILITY?

Typically the average stay for a patient in an acute rehab facility is approximately 20 days. It can vary from patient to patient depending on the diagnosis.

WILL MY GRANDMA RECOVER?

With the above mentioned therapies—in conjunction with the physicians, nurses, psychologists, nutritionists, case managers, social workers, and even music therapists working the patient's individual treatment plan—Grandma has an excellent chance of regaining most of her pre-hospitalization form.

Here is a typical scenario that a patient or family might see, which would result in a future Acute Inpatient Rehabilitation Facility admission:

Uncle George, a fifty-two-year-old male, has a history of high cholesterol, insulin dependent diabetes, and hypertension. He works in an oil refinery and started to have right-sided weakness on the job, slurred speech, and was rushed to the hospital with the aid of some co-workers. After going through the emergency room, he was admitted to the ICU as he recovered from having a stroke. After a couple of days in the ICU, Uncle George goes to the Telemetry Unit and is making some good progress but is still in need of extensive rehab and nursing care. The MDs and Case Manager/Social Worker contact the patient's wife to discuss sending Uncle George to an Acute Inpatient Rehabilitation Facility to continue his treatment and recovery.

QUESTIONS

_____
_____
_____
_____

NOTES

_____
_____
_____
_____

4
DAD HAS TO GO TO A "SNIFF?"

A "sniff," "SNF," or Skilled Nursing Unit is a medical facility that treats chronically ill patients who are sick enough to need around the clock care but not critical enough to require hospitalization. SNFs include rehabilitation, various medical procedures, and nursing care.

The ratio of nurse to patients is about 30 to 1, and doctors don't typically see the patients daily. They do need to be available on an emergency basis, and at least one RN (registered nurse) should be employed. This is vastly different from an LTACH, which is staffed just like a **traditional short-term acute care hospital.** The low nurse to high patient ratio and the physician availability are the main differences between LTACHs/IRFs and SNFs.

Most of the time, "sniffs" are located inside of nursing homes, and many elderly patients with long-standing illnesses transition from

SNFs to becoming permanent residents of nursing homes.

SNFs are one of the most common places to which patients are discharged after they become stable at the hospital. They cost about 1/3 as much as an LTACH and much less than a traditional hospital.

QUESTIONS

NOTES

5
ON THE ROAD TO RECOVERY…
OUTPATIENT REHABILITATION

Outpatient rehabilitation facilities are where patients travel to clinics to participate in timed sessions (about 30 minutes to an hour on average) and return home the same day. This is usually a very good sign. Patients who are admitted to outpatient rehab facilities are healing enough to go home, and the physicians feel good that patients can complete their therapies in an outpatient setting.

Most outpatient rehabs focus on three areas of treatment: Physical, Occupational, and Speech Therapy. Typically, these are the main ones that focus on the patient's ADLs (activities of daily living) but can be expanded after the initial treatment plan to include pain therapy, hand therapy, sleep disorders therapy, orthopedic therapy, aquatic therapy, and many others. Be sure to ask the doctors at the hospital for more information about the level of care.

QUESTIONS

_____

_____

_____

_____

NOTES

_____

_____

_____

_____

6
MOM CAN GO HOME WITH HOME HEALTH? WHAT'S THAT?

Home Health Companies allow patients to receive healthcare in the patient's home by Nurses, Medical Assistants, Physical Therapists, and other healthcare professionals. HHs (home health) provide professional services that can include wound care, pain management, IV therapy, physical therapy, speech therapy, psychological assessments, disease education, and ADLs. The patient has an assigned home health doctor, and they are in contact with the nurse or healthcare professional to discuss changes in the patient's condition and if any medications or treatments need to be changed.

Patients can and often are discharged home to HHs from traditional hospitals, LTACHs, SNFs, and just about all healthcare settings. In addition, if a person goes "home with home health," and while at home they don't respond to treatment, they can always be directly admitted back to the appropriate level of care, such as an LTACH or SNF, bypassing a return visit to the ER or traditional "med surg" unit.

QUESTIONS

_____

_____

_____

_____

NOTES

_____

_____

_____

_____

7
GRAMMY HAS TO GO TO A NURSING HOME NOW?

Nursing Homes can offer a variety of services but generally care for the chronically ill patients (elderly or younger patients with mental or physical disabilities) who need around the clock monitoring/nursing care. Services generally provided include medication administration and monitoring, personal care, 24/7 emergency care, room and board (single and double occupancy), and social/recreational activities.

The nursing home staff members are able to assess patients regularly and can have residents sent to the hospital in a very timely fashion if their condition warrants it. It's generally safer to be at a nursing home than for a patient to be home with a chronic health condition.

I recently had to put my ninety-one-year-old father in a nursing home, and it was the toughest thing I ever had to do. He had some new onset of dementia the last few years, and I could not continue to give him the care he needed and deserved. Just like the majority of people, I have to work full time. After much self-imposed guilt, I made the move, and he wasn't thrilled about it. To my surprise, it has been a blessing, and he has done very well and likes living there. He adjusted well, and I have the peace of mind that he is being cared for by dedicated healthcare professionals. He has his bad days, like all of us, but had I known he would have adjusted so well I would have done it a little sooner.

Do your homework and visit a few different nursing homes; you will eventually find the right one, as I did.

QUESTIONS

_____
_____
_____
_____

NOTES

_____
_____
_____

8
HOSPICE... IS IT REALLY THE END OF THE ROAD?

WHAT IS HOSPICE CARE?

Hospice care is for patients and their families who have had a long-standing illness (typically like cancer, but it can be any number of illnesses) and are nearing the end of life. Hospice care facilities typically provide healthcare in the patient's home and is made up of nurses, doctors, psychologists, social services, those who can supply spiritual guidance, and many other comfort measures. Pain management and maximizing comfort levels are the primary goals of Hospice care.

WHO BENEFITS FROM HOSPICE CARE?

Terminally ill patients who have six months or less to live often benefit from Hospice care. In many cases, patients who get Hospice care tend to live longer and develop stronger relationships with family members and the Hospice care professionals. Usually the experience is positive and rewarding for all involved.

WHO PAYS FOR HOSPICE CARE?

Most care is covered by Medicare, Medicaid, and Managed Care Insurance companies. It's always good to check with your healthcare provider to make sure you understand what the options are.

QUESTIONS

_____

_____

_____

_____

NOTES

_____

_____

_____

_____

9
ANOTHER OPTION?
ASSISTED LIVING

As noted before, my father is now ninety-one and living happily in a nursing home in New Orleans. When he was eighty-eight, I could see that he was beginning to slow down and needed more care. As we all know, it is difficult to work full time and take care of our elderly loved ones. As I tried to figure out what to do, I looked into "assisted living facilities" and what they could provide.

Assisted Living Facilities or Communities vary in different areas of the country but are generally viewed as one of the best options for aging seniors. The residents get assistance with basic ADLs (activities of daily living), and many seniors start with an independent living facility (which are usually considered any form of housing that targets seniors fifty-five and older). They then transition to assisted living or to nursing homes if their health declines to a point where that is needed.

I made a promise to take care of my dad as long as I could, and I did as good a job as I could with no help. He never did go to an assisted living place, and although it was tough for us both to have him go to a nursing home, it has worked out better than either of us could have imagined.

I have visited many assisted living facilities for my job in the healthcare industry, and just about all of them provide a great service to the elderly. We all have so much on our plates these days, and transitioning our grandparents and parents into these types of facilities helps to ensure their safety and gives them a good chance to get medical assistance quickly and to the right level of care when the situation arises.

In closing, I hope this pocket guide can serve as a tool helping you navigate the many different areas of healthcare and the places to which a patient can go after their visit to the hospital. The process for a patient to go to the next "post acute (PAC)" level of care can be a bit overwhelming at times. Use this guide to help family, friends and the patient understand the continuation of their medical treatment and care. Good luck!!

Glossary

LTACH   Long-term Acute Care Hospital

STACH   Short-term Acute Care Hospital

SNF   Skilled Nursing Unit

HH   Home Health

IRH   Inpatient Rehabilitation Hospital

PAC   Post Acute Care

OPF   Outpatient Rehabilitation Facility

NH   Nursing Home

Appendix

The following websites may be useful to the continued health and well-being of your family.

American Academy of Allergy, Asthma & Immunology
http://www.aaaai.org

American Autoimmune Related Diseases Association
http://www.aarda.org

American Cancer Society
http://www.cancer.org

American Diabetes Association
http://www.diabetes.org

American Gastroenterological Association
http://www.gastro.org

American Heart Association
http://americanheart.org

American Society of Dermatologic Surgery
http://www.asds-net.org

U.S. Food and Drug Administration
http://www.fda.gov

Lab Tests Online
http://www.labtestonline.org

March of Dimes Foundation
http://www.marchofdimes.com

Mayo Clinic
http://www.mayoclinic.com

National Cancer Institute
http://www.cancer.gov/

National Heart, Lung and Blood Institute
http://nhlbi.nih.gov

National Institute of Allergy and INFECTIOUS DISEASES
http://niaid.nih.gov

National Institute of Arthritis and Musculoskeletal and Skin Disease
http://www.niams.nih.gov

National Institute of Neurological Disorders and Stroke
http://www.ninds.gov/

www.ingramcontent.com/pod-product-compliance
Lightning Source LLC
Chambersburg PA
CBHW060645030426
42337CB00018B/3451